Self-Publishing on a Budget
with Amazon

A Guide for the Author Publishing eBooks on
Kindle

Jill b.

ISBN: 1519153821
ISBN-13: 978-1519153821

CONTENTS

1 INTRODUCTION

I have to be honest. I never dreamt of being an author, self-published or otherwise. It started with the death of a beloved chicken, that led to the reinvention of the chicken saddle. Since we had a shoe-string budget, I marketed the saddle by pitching stories and articles to niche chicken-keeping and homesteading magazines on speculation. Some stories were accepted and published but I also saw my rejection pile starting to grow.

It was then that my husband suggested that I turn the information I had previously written into a book - *How to Keep Backyard Chickens* (available at http://byjillb.com). I've since self-published nine books. This will be the tenth. It is a book that I didn't plan to write but is one that called to me and one that now needs to be written.

This is not a motivational or a marketing book. This book is not about how anyone can write a book or why you should write a book. I will not extol the virtues of writing and self-publishing. This is not a get-rich-quick scheme book. Everyone's journey is different. Even if you followed J.K. Rowling or Stephen King's writing journey to a T, your outcome will be different.

Beware of snake oil salesman who will promise indie authors the world. Self-publishing is like any business. Some people go on to sell millions of books. Other authors may sell none. There is no magic sauce. What works for one author will not necessarily work for another.

Everybody's journey is different. There are indeed quite a lot of indie authors who have made a good living from their books. Some, like the likes of Amanda Hocking and John Locke have made a lot of money. Again, this is not a get-rich-quick book.

I will not promise you fame and fortune if you follow my steps and ideas. Instead, the intention of this book is to help beginning self-publishing authors to navigate through the world of self-publishing, as cheaply as possible without sacrificing quality. This book is not about cheating your readers. It is about working as best as you can with what you have to publish a book within reasonable means.

2 WHY DO YOU WANT TO SELF-PUBLISH?

Before you continue down the self-publishing road, you need to know *why* you want to self-publish your book. Without a clear reason for wanting to write and self-publish a book, you may end up lost without even realizing it.

There is no wrong answer as to why you want to self-publish. Maybe you simply want to get your story or message out into the world. Maybe you've already tried the traditional publishing route and want to try something else. Maybe you want to publish a book to improve your business reputation, make money or perhaps to keep full control and maximum royalties for your work. There are many reasons why someone decides to self-publish. Being clear as to what *your* reasons are will help to provide you with a focus as you write, market and brand your book, as well as yourself.

As you think about your reasons, also keep an open mind - your reasons may change over time as you learn and grow as an author and self-publisher. When I wrote my first book on *How to Keep Backyard Chickens*, my main reasons for self-publishing were

- to produce a potential sales funnel for my chicken saddles
- to write a book which covered topics which I felt that beginner chicken guides failed to discuss
- to produce a source of passive income.

When my first book was completed, I started reading and learning about marketing my ebook. I stumbled on KBoards Writers' Cafe (http://kboards.com), a supportive and active forum for indie authors. It was then that I discovered that it is possible to earn a good income from writing and self-publishing books.

Learning from others that came before me, I decided that my best marketing tactic and the best way to create a larger passive income source would be to write more books in popular genres. Luckily for me, topics like home-based businesses, homesteading and gardening are popular and right up my alley. If money is not your motivation, feel free to skip parts of this book.

3 SELF-PUBLISHING - WHAT TO EXPECT

Can you make some extra money on the side through self-publishing? Absolutely.

Can you earn a living through self-publishing? Definitely.

Can you get rich through self-publishing? Maybe.

The road to self-publication can be long and hard. It can be a steep learning curve. This is not to say that going the traditional publishing route is easy either. However, as a self-publisher, you will have to wear many hats, which may include formatter, cover designer, book editor, copy editor, web designer and marketing manager (which may include social media and search engine optimization) in *addition* to being an author.

Depending on your book, your reasons for self-publishing, your budget and your aptitude, you may outsource some or all of the above jobs. The less you spend on production, the easier it will be for you to turn a profit on your book, if that is your intention.

4 WORD PROCESSING

Many authors use Microsoft Word. The software is, however, not free. If you do not already have it, you can use free word processing software like Google Docs (http://drive.google.com) or Open Office (http://openoffice.org). I personally use Google Docs because it is not only free, it automatically saves your work onto the Google cloud every few minutes.

Other word processing options include Scrivener, Zotero and Wordpress. If you feel more comfortable dictating your book rather than typing it, you can consider using Dragon Speaking Naturally, which is a speech-to-text software. While I will discuss the basics of each word processing option, the details go beyond the scope of this book.

Google Docs

I have used MS Word in the past, and have lost large amounts of work due to system malfunctions. Since then, I've found Google Docs (http://docs.google.com) to be a lifesaver many times over. Not only does Google Docs save your work automatically, you can also access all your work from any computer, anywhere in the world.

You can even share your work-in-progress with anyone you wish, including editors and proofreaders. Collaborators can view the document in real time and make real-time changes to the document. To share your document with collaborators, click on the "File" button in the top menu and select "Email Collaborators" in the drop-down menu. You can then enter the email address of your collaborator. At this time, you can also choose the permissions for your collaborator - either allowing them to edit, comment or merely to allow them to view the document.

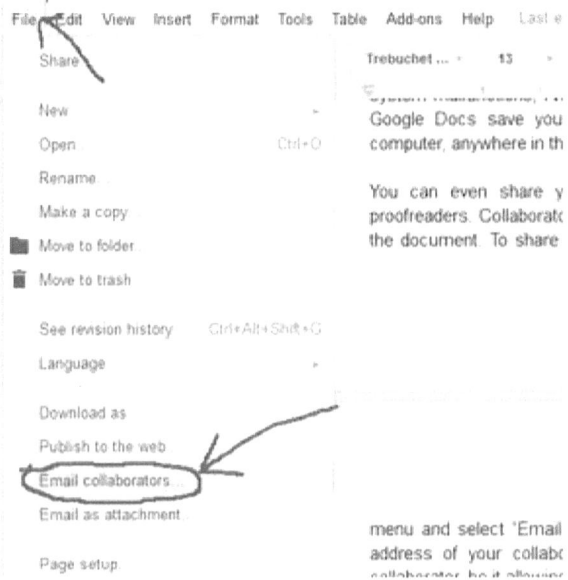

Wordpress

Wordpress (http://wordpress.com) was originally designed for blogging. However, some authors also use it for word processing. Like Google Docs, your files are saved in Wordpress rather than on your computer, which makes it very convenient to access from anywhere on any computer.

Like Google Docs, you can also invite collaborators to read or edit your manuscript in real time. You can invite collaborators by clicking on the "SHARING" button on the menu on the right side of the page. Wordpress leaves you the option of saving your work on your own time rather than auto-saving like Google Docs does.

Some additional plus sides to using Wordpress for word processing include being able tag your work as well as to post your work on social media sites in a more streamlined fashion.

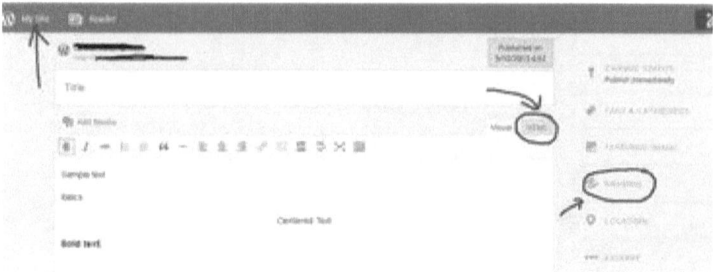

Wordpress also provides a HTML tab just above your text box which allows you to view the HTML format styling with little fuss. I will discuss the importance of HTML in the chapter on formatting.

The downside to using Wordpress is that can be more prone to hacking than Google. However, you might find that the additional functions that suit your needs may be worth the potential risk.

Scrivener

Many authors swear by Scrivener (http://hyperurl.co/scrivener), which is a word processor designed specifically for authors. Scriver allows you to compose text on virtual index cards, allowing you to move them around to piece the perfect sequence.

Scrivener also allows you to keep all your research material including "images, PDF files, movies, web pages [and] sound files" within the program and allows you to view them alongside each other.

The software is available at http://hyperurl.co/scrivener for $40. However, keep an eye out for their 50% off sale which Scrivener may run during the pre or post Christmas season (usually starting the day after Thanksgiving in the US).

Zotero

Often used by academics to create their own research reference libraries, Zotero (https://www.zotero.org/) is a free, open source software that has research capabilities similar to Scrivener. It allows you to store snapshots of any web page as well as store online .pdf files for easy future access. It will also integrate with other word processing software like MS Word, allowing you to more easily access your references.

Dragon Naturally Speaking

For the writer who feels more comfortable dictating rather than typing, Dragon Naturally Speaking software is one of the best speech-to-text software currently available. The software learns and adapts to you so you will need to spend some time "training" the Dragon. The software retails for $99 and isn't the cheapest to buy. However, the older version is available on Amazon for about $30-40.

If you are in the US and are in no hurry to get it, you can also get Dragon for free or close to free after rebate. Go to SlickDeals (http://slickdeals.net), a forum which features crowdsourced deals. Type in "Dragon Naturally" in the search box to see if there are any current deals. If there aren't any at the moment, set up an alert for when a deal does come up. Slickdeals will then notify you via email when a deal crops up.

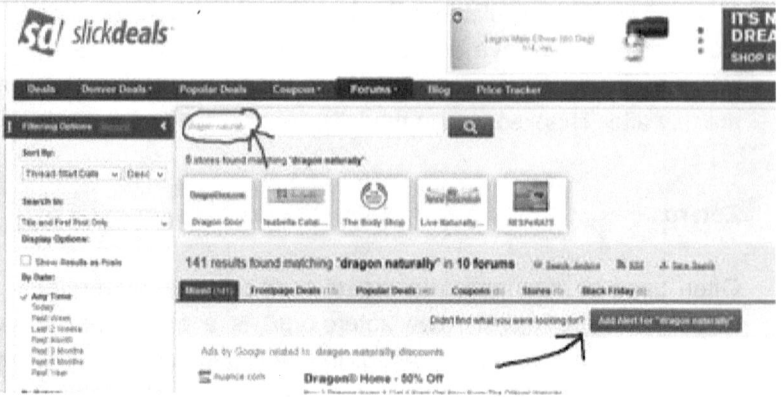

5 WRITING YOUR BOOK

This is not an instructional writing book. Writing for different genres varies widely and it would be impossible for me to cover the nuances of writing in each and every genre. My best advice on writing would be to be widely read before you write.

Fortunately, most writers would already have this crucial step completed by the time they reach their teens. It helps to be widely read, but you need not necessarily need to read deeply into your genre. That is, you do not need to read thousands of romance books in order to write a romance novel. You should, however, read a number of books within your chosen genre so that you can get a "feel" of how books in that particular genre are usually written. Develop your own voice to write within your niche.

If you are unsure where to start, download books from the Bestselling List in your genre. Sign up with BookBub (http://bookbub.com) to get informed about free or discounted highly-rated e-books.

If you'd like to brush up on your English skills, or if you want to learn more about fiction writing, you can sign up for free online courses at Futurelearn (https://www.futurelearn.com) or Coursera (http://coursera.org). Different courses are run by different universities or cultural institutions like the British Council.

If you'd like to boost your writing confidence, consider writing smaller works for publications. Refer to New Pages (http://www.newpages.com) for a current listing of submission calls. If you are a non-fiction writer and writing a whole book seems daunting, consider flexing your writing muscles by first pitching and writing some articles to magazines within your area of expertise.

Pitching to smaller publications is usually easier as the publisher/editor is usually less inundated with submission queries and may be more likely to respond to you. For example, I have written articles for various magazines including Backyard Poultry Magazine, Countryside and Small Stock Journal, Rocky Mountain Gardening Magazine. The magazines are small and niche but were accessible and covered topics within my area of interest and expertise.

Look for magazines that you might be able to write for at book stores or even on grocery store magazine racks. Go over the magazines that catch your eye so that you can get a feel of the magazine's audience and voice. Write your article in that voice. You may even get paid while you hone your skills!

Start writing your book as soon as you feel comfortable enough to do so. The first draft doesn't have to be perfect. I've found that sitting down and writing helps to keep the words flowing. Many indie authors on Kboards who write for a living aim to write at least 1,000 words per day. Others prefer to set a time frame in which chapters are completed. Regardless of your yardstick, setting a goal gives you a concrete number versus time line to meet and helps to keep you on track to finish your book within a reasonable time frame.

I admit that with two small children at home, homeschooling, homesteading and running another business, I'm not always able to meet the 1,000 word daily count. However, I do try my best to write at least *something* almost everyday.

I've been able to publish 9 books in 5 months because of this daily word goal. Of course, non-fiction books tend to be shorter than fiction. If you write epic fantasy books, it'll probably take you longer to release your book. Again, there is no right or wrong method, only the method that works for you and your situation.

6 EDITING

After you've finished writing your book, it'll need to be edited. Self-editing can be a hot-topic issue amongst indie authors. Some insist that you cannot edit your own work. I, on the other hand, believe that while some people cannot necessarily edit their own work, just like some people cannot design nice book covers, others can.

Depending on how versed you are in your genre and depending on your language aptitude, you may or may not wish to hire an editor. If you're strapped for cash but need to hire an editor, consider bartering something of value with someone who is qualified to edit your work.

You can also consider joining a writing critique group like Scribophile (http://scribophile.com) or Critique.org (http://critique.org), both of which welcome writers of most mainstream genres, Critters Writers (http://critters.org) for Science Fiction/ Fantasy/ Horror writers or Book Country (http://bookcountry.com), which is a peer critique website.

Developmental Editing

Possibly one of the more expensive editors is a developmental editor who will guide a writer from idea to the final product. They may come up with book concepts or make big changes to the final draft including making changes to improve coherence, plot, structure, characters and overall flow of the book.

Content Editing

A content editor is someone who helps the big picture of your book. For example, a content editor will help point out any plot holes, areas that may need to be expanded on, any part that may be unclear or that may need to be removed as well as content that may need to be moved to another part of the book. Fiction generally benefits more from content editing than non-fiction.

Copy Editing

A copy editor basically goes over your manuscript with a fine-toothed comb, checking for redundancies or helping with better word choices. He/she will also fix spelling and grammatical errors or may reword and improve sentence structure.

Proof-Reader

Even though proofreading sometimes gets confused with copy editing, the two are not necessarily one and the same. A proofreader will go over the final edited manuscript draft, looking for any possible typos, spelling or punctuation errors. They may also correct the use of regionally incorrect English. They may for example, ensure that the manuscript is uniformly written in American or British English.

Beta-Readers

Beta-readers are usually non-professional readers who will read your book before it is published. They may give you insights as to what they what they thought of the book, plot, characters or overall story.

Some may help to correct any factual mistakes for example, if you named a gun or car model incorrectly. Beta-readers may or may not point out and/or correct typos, spelling or grammatical errors and often do not charge for their help.

Editing Costs

Having your book edited is one of the largest expenses when it comes to self-publishing. Editors charge an average of $0.005 per word, with developmental editors usually charging more. Obviously, the longer your book, the higher your editing costs. You can refer to the Editorial Freelancers Association website at http://hyperurl.co/editrate for an idea of expected current editorial rates.

Where to Find Editors

Besides using your own network to find an editor, consider first asking writers in your genre whom you respect for recommendations. Other places to get recommendations include Writer's Digest (http://writersdigest.com), World Literary Cafe (http://worldliterarycafe.com) or on KBoards Writer's Cafe (http://kboards.com). Look for recommendations, not merely ads posted by the editor.

While I don't recommend this option, you can also look for an editor on Elance (http://elance.com), Odesk (http://odesk.com), Fiverr (http://fiverr.com) or on KBoards (http://kboards.com/yp).

If you're unable to find an editor that suits to your needs, you can also post job requests on Elance, Odesk and Fiverr. To request a gig on Fiverr, you will need to log into your Fiverr account and choose the "Request A Gig" button under "My Orders".

It is a little easier to post a job on Elance or Odesk. Simply use the "Post a Job" button to submit your job request. State what kind of job you're looking for, for example "Copy Editor" or "Developmental Editor" or "Proofreader".

Look for someone with an eye for detail with excellent literary skills and with experience in the kind of editing that you need. State -

- The kind of book you are writing
- A short synopsis of what the book is about
- Word count
- The dateline with which you need to have your book completely edited by
- The level and kind of editing you need done
- If you need American or British English editing
- Editing for any other regional English dialects. For example Irish, Scottish, Australian or other Commonwealth speakers of English may not necessary have the same dialog style.

To help you to filter out proposals, state that all queries need to include a phrase of your choosing, for example, you can include the request that all submissions should be titled "My Crazy Chicken". This way, you can save *your* time by filtering out anyone who did not or cannot follow instructions.

Once you have narrowed your choices down, most editors should be willing to send you a sample edit of your work. Send all of them the same sample copy to edit. This way, you can compare their work. Remember that hiring an editor does not relieve you of having to know proper grammar, sentence structure and punctuation rules. You need to know the language rules in order to know if the editor has correctly edited your manuscript or not. A good editor can make your work sing. A bad one can butcher your work.

Finally, your editor should have an interest in the genre you're writing in. Ask your editor to give you a list of books in your genre that they have edited. Amazon is usually the best place to look for that book's reviews. When looking at the book's reviews, look out for low ratings as they pertain to editing. It is a big red flag if the editor's books are getting a lot of bad reviews about editing.

Once you've found an editor that you like, make sure that both parties can agree on price and terms. Do not hire them if there is any point of contention. Remember that your editor is *not* your ghost writer or co-author. Your manuscript should be as clean as possible before you hand it off to your editor.

Pareto's 80-20 Rule: Do-It-Yourself

According to Wikipedia, Italian economist Vilfredo Pareto, theorized the 80-20 Rule in 1896. In essence, the Rule theorizes that 80% of the output comes from 20% of the effort. From an indie publishing point of view, that will mean that you will have to spend 80% of your time (and money) to get that last 20% of perfection out of your book. Of course, there is no "perfect" book, even if you have multiple people edit and correct your book.

I decided to self-edit when my first books were returned to me with very few corrections. Using the 80-20 Rule, I decided from a business standpoint that it was no longer cost-effective for me to enlist the services of an editor.

I edit as I write, then do a final edit when the draft is finished. If you feel more comfortable having at least *something* else giving your manuscript a once over, services like ProWritingAid, (http://prowritingaid.com), Grammarly (https://www.grammarly.com/) and AutoCrit (https://www.autocrit.com/) can help to correct and possibly improve your prose. ProWritingAid offers a free service that will run up to 3000 words for free. They also offer a lifetime "pro" subscription for $120. The other services charge between $60 to $140 per year. Grammarly also offers monthly subscriptions.

That said, genre matters. Readers of some genres may be more picky than readers of others. I write non-fiction books and as long as I can convey my ideas and information in a clear enough manner, the 80-20 Rule applies. Self-edit according to how comfortable you feel about your ability and your budget.

7 FORMATTING

Formatting should always be done *after* your book is edited. You'll need to format it for digital publication, which is different from a print format. If you want to upload on Amazon, which is currently the largest sales platform for most self-publishers, you'll need to have a .mobi file.

Regardless of the publishing format, you will usually start with a .doc file. If you're publishing to the Kindle using Microsoft Word, Amazon has a free book available at http://hyperurl.co/amzformat on how to properly format your work.

The main rule for formatting for digital publication is to use the correct word processor functions so that the document can be more properly read during conversion.

Table of Contents

Your Kindle publications must have a Table of Contents. This is especially important for non-fiction How-To books because Amazon has a "Look Inside" feature which shows the first 10% of a book. Your reader will be looking for content topics covered within the book.

Each word processor has slightly different options. However, the function to insert the Table of Contents should generally be the same. To insert your Table of Contents using Google Docs, place your cursor key in the part of the manuscript where you want to place your Table of Contents in. Click on the "insert" button on the top menu

and select "Table of Contents". The same method applies to adding page breaks.

Chapter Headings

In order to properly generate your Table of Contents, you have to use proper headers for your headings. To make chapter and sub-chapter headers, highlight the chapter headers and choose the header option, using "Heading 1" or <h1> in HTML code for the main chapter heading. Use "Heading 2" for sub-chapters.

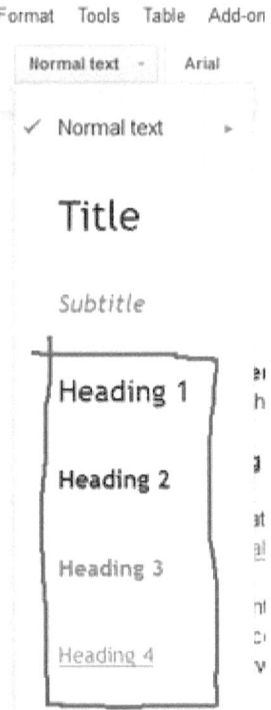

When the chapter headings are appropriately generated, your table of contents will look something like this on the Kindle:

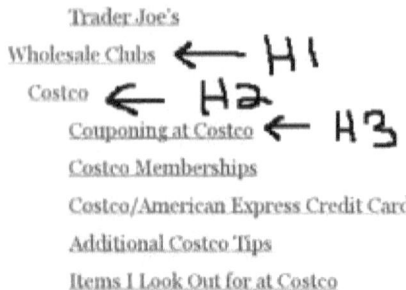

Setting Fonts and Page Numbers

Since readers can set their own fonts and font size on their reader, there is no need to worry too much about fonts in your formatting. I like to use the neutral "Arial" font when I'm word-processing. Similarly, digital books are not numbered by page since the page number will change depending on the reader's settings. Therefore, there is no need to number your pages.

Adding Links

Being able to add live web links to your e-books is a nice feature to have, especially when you're writing some non-fiction genres. Some people choose to simply add the link to the word or word phrase, similar to the format found on websites.

I've chosen to streamline my formatting process for both digital and print publication by including the URL as a live link next to the text. Including a text link within the book also makes it easier for readers using older Kindle models to check out the sites that you are referencing.

Unfortunately, many links may look like this:

https://itunes.apple.com/us/artist/jill-b./id965454621?mt=11&uo=4&a t=10lSme or longer. Use a URL shortener to neaten the look of your text. Many authors like using Bitly (http://bitly.com). By entering your long URL into the shortener, this link, https://itunes.apple.com/us/artist/jill-b./id965454621?mt=11&uo=4&a t=10lSme will be shortened to this: http://apple.co/1BYeia7

Tiny URL (http://tinyurl.com) offers a shortening service similar to Bitly. The service I've come to like the most, however, is SmartURL (http://smarturl.it) because you can not only customize the shortened URL, you can keep track of all your shortened links within your SmartURL account.

SmartURL turns this long URL link https://itunes.apple.com/us/artist/jill-b./id965454621?mt=11&uo=4&a t=10lSme to a neater, customized link that looks like this: http://hyperurl.co/jillbitunes.

Default URL

smartURL will send traffic to this URL if the visitor is from an uns and country.

ADD URL HERE

Country Destinations

smartURL will override the default URL, and forward the visitor to specific destination.

Country	URL

Device Destinations

smartURL will override the default URL, and forward the visitor to destination.

Device	URL
Android	
-- Select -- ∨	

Organize (Optional)

Custom Alias

smarturl.it/

hyperurl.co/ CUSTOM URL

Once you have formatted your manuscript, save it as a .doc or .docx to upload it onto Amazon's Kindle Direct Publishing (http://kdp.amazon.com).

HTML

Bear in mind that unless you are working in a HTML file, the .doc or .docx file that we created is likely to have bugs. All word processors use underlying HTML code to make it look good when it's printed. However, this same HTML code can also get mangled when it is converted to .mobi. or .epub for digital publishing.

If talk of HTML and CSS computer coding makes your eyes glaze over, I prescribe the 80-20 Rule since this is a book about publishing on a budget. Format your book within your word processor and move on to the next chapter.

Remember that even the Kindle is not just the Kindle. There are many Kindle models ranging from the first generation Kindles to the Paperwhite to the Kindle Fires. Add the multitudes of other reading devices and you can understand why each and every reader may not display your manuscript as you intended it to unless you have it properly coded in HTML. You can use Wordpress' HTML option to help you to generate your HTML. However, it would still be helpful if you learned some basic code. Refer to http://w3schools.com for free tutorials.

If you want to properly format your book with HTML, I suggest using Adobe's free open source software, Brackets (http://brackets.io/) which you can use together with Google Chrome (http://google.com/chrome). Google Chrome will allow you to see how your manuscript looks in a browser as you work. Save the completed, scripted manuscript in .html format.

Save the .html file together with all the image files used in that book in a compressed zip folder. To generate a zip folder, right-click your mouse on the desktop. Select "New" and select "Compressed (zipped) Folder" to create a new zip

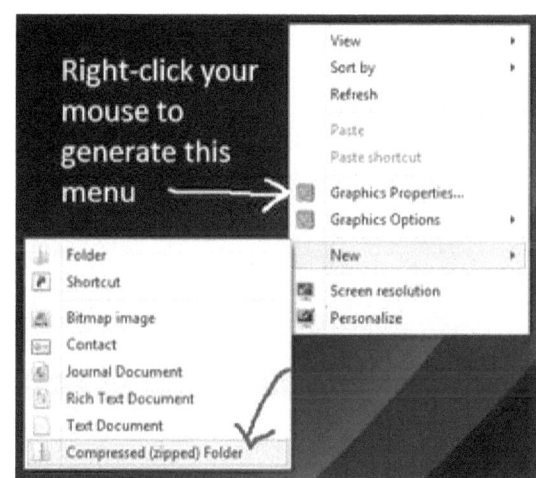

file. I've included a snapshot of what the process should look like but the layout may vary depending on your operating system.

You can then upload the compressed file and convert it for free using Calibre (http://calibre-ebook.com/). If you'd like to learn more about e-book formatting, you can refer to Guido Henkel's *The Zen eBook Formatting*. Mr Henkel has also kindly put large exerpts of his book on his blog which you can read for free at http://hyperurl.co/properformat.

If all this coding talk is too much to digest and if you have a little bit of a budget to pay someone to do it for you, I suggest hiring someone on Fiverr. I've used seller kindle_format (https://www.fiverr.com/kindle_format) with good results. Polgarus Studios (http://www.polgarusstudio.com) charges a little more but is another formatter recommended by top selling indie authors like Hugh Howey.

8 COVERS

"Don't judge a book by its cover" - English idiom

Much as I'd like to say that people don't judge a book by its cover, they do. Sorry, but in order to sell your book, packaging matters. You will need to have a nice cover that is appropriate for your genre. My non-fiction how-to genre is more forgiving. Other genres like fantasy require more elaborate covers.

Again, the best way to get a feel of what the covers of books in your genre should look like, refer to your genre's best seller list on Amazon. You can refer to bestseller list on other platforms but I've found that other platforms tend to feature more books that are traditionally published on their best seller lists.

Take note of traditionally published book covers but also remember that many of their covers were designed to look good on a regular-sized book. Unfortunately, many traditional cover designs do not shrink well when it is viewed in an image the size of a postage stamp - that is the e-book platform's thumbnail image of your book's cover.

Be Your Target Audience

It is not always easy to step out of your own shoes but put yourself in the shoes of your target *audience* (not yourself) before deciding on what works or does not work for your cover. For example, when my husband was helping with the cover design for my *Modern American Frugal Housewife* Series, we initially decided to feature the human evolution chart on the cover, with a female Victorian silhouette (an homage to the author of the original book, Maria Lydia Child) and then a modern-day woman at the end of the graphic.

Fortunately we were able to step out of our shoes before the cover was completed because we remembered that a large portion of readers for this series may be conservatively Christian. A cover like that would possibly alienate a big part of our readership. We back-tracked and settled on an all-text cover.

Cover Text

Remember that your book cover's size on a screen will approximately be the size of a postage stamp. Avoid making covers that are too busy. The main cover text should be bold and easy to read. Avoid using fancy fonts and effects. The general rule is to stick to no more than two font styles.

You want a cover that conveys the message of the book to the reader immediately. In general, fiction book covers should speak to the reader's emotions and a nonfiction book should speak to the reader's head. Non-fiction memoir covers may fall into either category. Depending on your genre, your author name may be small or big and bold.

If designing your own cover seems daunting, you book cover designs start at $5 from Fiverr (http://fiverr.com). In my view, $5 Fiverr covers are more suitable if you need a simple, non-fiction book cover. For fiction book covers on a budget, you may be better off buying a pre-made cover. Pre-made covers usually start at around $35. Again, you can refer to http://www.kboards.com/yp/ for cover designer listings.

Alternatively, if there is a cover design on an independently published book that you think will help to sell your books, you can try contacting the author for their cover designer information. Some books may even list the cover designer in the acknowledgements (see if you can find this information in Amazon's "Look Inside" feature by clicking on the image of the book).

Make sure that your cover designer has purchased commercial rights to use any images featured on your book cover. You should also clarify what kind of rights you have to the cover design before finalizing the order. Some licenses may not be transferrable. That is, while the designer may have purchased use image rights, the license might not allow them to purchase the image, design a book cover, and in turn sell that cover to you. To err on the side of caution, some authors prefer to purchase image licensing rights and have the designer use the images that they (the author) purchased to design their cover.

Again there is no right or wrong way to go about designing your cover. If you're on a tight budget, you can always opt to design a cover yourself first, then buy a cover when you can afford it.

Do-It-Yourself

There are many design softwares that will design a cover for you. For completeness, I have to add that Amazon has a Cover Creator where you can design a very simple cover within the Kindle Direct Publishing (KDP) when you upload your manuscript. However, unless you have a creative streak, Amazon's Cover Creator will produce a very simple but generally ugly cover.

If you need photos for your cover, you might be able to find public domain photos or photos available for commercial use for free on Wikimedia Commons (http://hyperurl.co/wikicom). You can also try searching for photos on Flickr (http://flickr.com). Search "The Commons" that can be found under the "Explore" button on the menu. Alternatively, you can search for photos by subject matter using the search box. You can then narrow down the searches by license (found in the submenu located under the main top menu). You can use some photos for commercial use for free. However, most commercial-use photos do not allow modification.

Here is a list of websites compiled by Shopify that offer free photos for commercial use from the following websites:

- Bucketlistly (http://photos.bucketlistly.com/)
- Cupcake (http://cupcake.nilssonlee.se/)
- Foodie's Feed (http://foodiesfeed.com/)
- Getrefe (http://getrefe.tumblr.com/)
- Gratisography (http://www.gratisography.com)
- ISO Republic (http://isorepublic.com/)
- Jay Mantri (http://jaymantri.com/)
- Life of Pix (http://www.lifeofpix.com/)
- MMT (http://mmt.li/)
- Pexels (http://www.pexels.com/)
- Picography (http://picography.co/)
- Pixabay (http://pixabay.com)
- Raumrot (http://www.raumrot.com/)
- Re:Splashed (http://www.resplashed.com/)
- SplitShire (http://splitshire.com/)
- Stok Pic (http://stokpic.com/)
- Startup Stock Photos (http://startupstockphotos.com/)
- Stock Snap (https://stocksnap.io/)
- SuperFamous (http://superfamous.com/)

Regardless of where you get your photos from, make sure that you properly attribute each photo according to the photo's attribution requirement.

Alternatively, Dollar Photo Club (http://dollarphotoclub.com) sells high resolution photos and illustrations for $1 each. You are allowed to use the photos that you buy for commercial use. *Update: Dollar Photo Club is no longer open to new members. You can instead buy photos from Adobe Stock (https://stock.adobe.com/) but images now cost $10 each.*

To edit photos, you can use free photo editing software from Pixlr (http://pixlr.com), PicMonkey (http://picmonkey.com) or Gimp (http://gimp.com).

Note that fonts and font color choice can make or break your cover design. Change them up until you produce a combination that looks good. If you need fonts for your cover, you can download fonts from 1001fonts (http://1001fonts.com) or dafont (http://dafont.com). Many but not all fonts are free for commercial use so make sure to filter your search appropriately before you download and use any particular font.

Because your e-book covers will be seen at approximately the size of a postage stamp, it's a good idea to use simple bold fonts that are easy to read when reduced in size. Script fonts tend to be too thin to be read easily. Avoid the urge to use fanciful fonts, especially if they are pictorial in nature.

Putting Your Cover Together

I am lucky to have a husband who is able to put a nice cover together. He originally used Adobe our ancient Photoshop and Illustrator earlier from earlier business endeavors. If you have a knack for design, the entire suite is now available on the Creative Cloud (http://adobe.com). Prices start at $9.99/month for Photoshop to $49.99/month for all the Adobe programs. There is quite an expense and learning curve to using Photoshop and Illustrator so I don't recommend using them in the beginning unless you know what you're doing.

If I, as an artistically-challenged author, had to design a cover myself on a budget, I recommend using Canva (http://canva.com), which has e-book cover design templates that are either free or cost $1 each. It utilizes a simple drag-and-drop interface which is very helpful for the technologically and design-challenged indie author. Signing up using your existing Facebook or Google Plus account is a simple process.

Canva's interface may change over time but basically, to design your cover on Canva, click on the "More" button under the "Create a design" section on the first page.

1. Click on the "Kindle cover" option to design your cover using the appropriate Kindle cover dimensions.

2. Choose your layout. If you are on a very tight budget, choose the free layout options which are denoted by the little "free" icon. You can click on any of the design elements to change, drag or remove them.

3. Customize your cover by changing the font style (again, opt for the free options if you are on a very tight budget).

4. You can also customize your design by changing the background.

5. Finally, for specific customization, you can upload your own images to add to your design. The images you upload can be your own, or can be images that you acquired from any other source, including those that I suggested in the earlier chapter. Canva will save your design as you go along. All the saved designs are easily accessible on your personal Canva homepage.

6. When you're satisfied with the final design, you can download it for free in either jpg or pdf format. If you used Canva's premium elements, you will be charged $1 per element used.

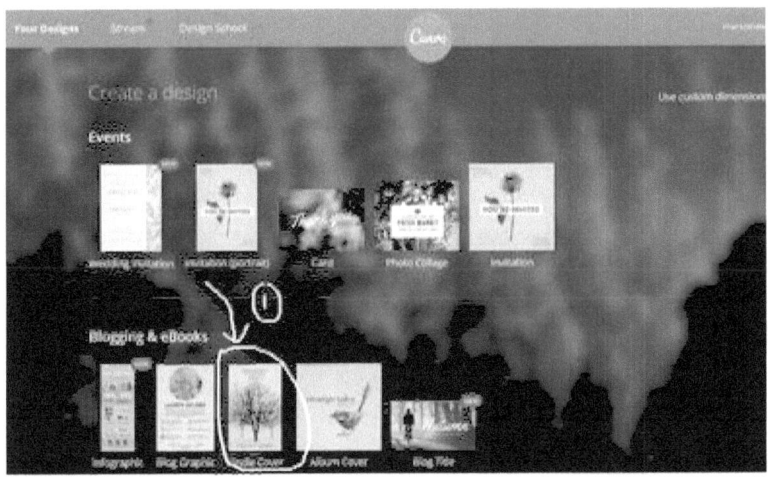

If you are interested in learning more about e-book cover design, refer to Jason Gurley's blog for free at http://hyperurl.co/diybookcover.

Calibre

Once you have your cover and your formatted book, you'll need to put it all together for digital publishing. Calibre has various functions but the basic function that you want out of the software is for it to convert your file into digital publishing formats. If you are not using a .doc file, you will need to use a .mobi file to upload your file onto Amazon Kindle Direct Publishing (KDP).

To do that,

1. Upload your book file by using the "Add books" button.
2. Click on "Convert books" to convert your books.
3. Make sure that you select .mobi format when preparing your file conversion. You can convert more than one book at a time by clicking on the book that you want to convert from you list of uploaded titles, then holding down the "Shift" button to select additional books at the same time.
4. Download your converted file onto your desktop for uploading onto Amazon KDP. Calibre will also allow you to preview your converted file if you click on the link next to the "Path", which can be found two lines under the "format" link.

If you prefer to double check your .epub file, you can also upload your file to an online validator at http://validator.idpf.org/.

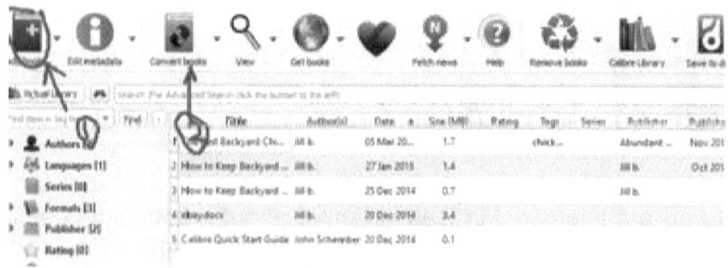

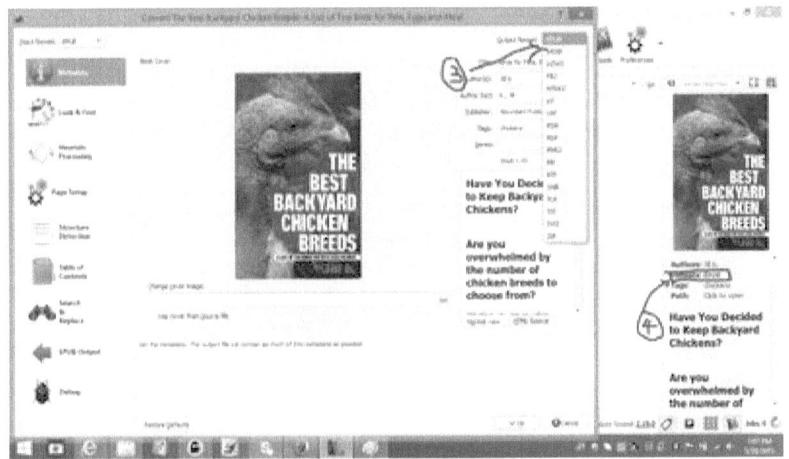

9 PUBLISHING ON AMAZON

Amazon currently has the biggest share in the US digital publishing market so it makes sense to consider publishing on Amazon first, before all others. To publish, you'll first need to set up a publishing account at http://kdp.amazon.com/.

You can sign up using your existing Amazon account but I suggest setting up a separate account for publishing so that you can keep your publishing business (if that's what you intend your books to become) separate from your personal Amazon account. You are only allowed to have **one** KDP account. However, you can have any number of pen names.

Before you can publish your book, you'll need to enter all your information, including your tax information.

If you are based in the US, you can choose to get paid via check, electronic funds transfer (EFT) or wire transfer. Many banks charge incoming wire transfer fees so I suggest using the EFT option which doesn't incur deposit fees. The funds are deposited into your bank account, meaning that you do not have to wait for a check to arrive in the mail then wait again for the bank to clear it.

Uploading Your Book to Amazon

Once you've setup your account, you can upload your book to be published! To publish, click on the "Bookshelf" button in the top menu. Click "Create a new title" to begin.

Book Descriptions

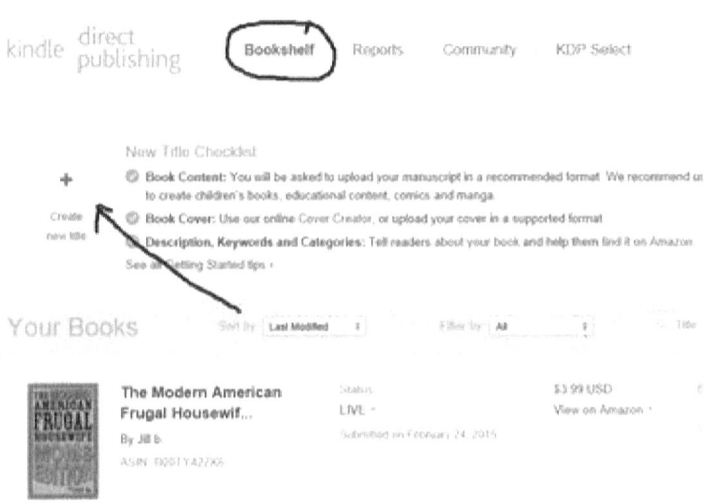

In the appropriate fields, check if you wish to enroll in the Select program, enter your book title, subtitle, edition number and publisher (if applicable), book description, contributors (add at least your author name in this field), language (the default is English), ISBN (leave it blank if you don't have one and Amazon will assign one to your book), publishing rights, categories (you can add up to two on Amazon), keywords and finally, your cover and book contents.

Some of the blanks that you need to fill are straightforward. However, there are a few parts of the uploading process that deserve special note. Specifically the Select program, the categories section, the book description and the keywords section.

Kindle Direct Publishing Select (KDP)

The KDP Select program is an optional program run by Amazon that demands publishing exclusivity for 90 days for any book that you enroll in the program. At the time of writing, being in Select allows you to offer your book for free for up to 5 days within that 90-day period, *or* to schedule one Countdown offer during the 90-day time-frame.

The Countdown offer allows you to offer you book at a discounted price (normally $0.99) for up to 7 days. You can then choose to increase the price incrementally over this 7 days, or you may opt to keep it at the $0.99 (or whatever price you choose) over the full 7 day offer. Amazon normally pays a 35% royalty rate on books priced at $0.99. However, if you opted for the 70% rate on a book regularly priced at $2.99-$9.99, you will continue to receive the 70% rate during the discounted countdown period.

Based on other author reports as well as my experience, it's more effective to keep the price at $0.99 over the entire Countdown period, rather than to gradually increase the price during the Countdown period. Sales tend to be more lacklustre as the price goes up, cutting into your precious promotion time. Again, every book is different so feel free to experiment with each new book!

If you choose instead to sign up for Select's free-day promotion option, Amazon will allow you to offer you book for free for 5 days. Your free days may be consecutive or nonconsecutive. I've found that it's best to offer free days for 2 or 3 consecutive days, especially if you've invested in some advertising. One free day tends to be too short and more than 3 days tends to be too long. Generally, it's best not to run free days on Fridays, Saturdays or big sporting event days when most people are not looking for books to download.

Why would you offer your book for free? The answer is exposure and visibility. Free days help to improve your visibility and download rate. This is especially important during the 30 days of the book's release, when Amazon helps to give your book a visibility boost. If you get enough downloads, your book can end up on the "Hot New Release" section, giving once again giving it more visibility.

Another advantage to offering your book for free is that it gives your book a chance to get reviews organically. Not everyone will read their free book download, nor will everyone leave a review. A general consensus which tallies with my own experience, is that you can expect to get an average of about 1 review per 1000 books downloaded.

Amazon also offers a paid advertising program however, by all current accounts, it does not yet seem to be an effective form of marketing. If you are on a budget, I suggest skipping this option unless something within Amazon's algorithm changes down the road.

Kindle Unlimited

At the time of writing, I think the main advantage of joining Select is the ability to loan your book out to subscribers of Amazon's Prime and Kindle Unlimited programs. Prime members are allowed to borrow one Select book per month. However, most authors do not see much of a borrow rate increase from Prime borrows.

Kindle Unlimited on the other hand, may boost your bottom line significantly. In a nutshell, subscribers pay Amazon a monthly subscription fee (currently $9.99/month) to join Kindle Unlimited. In return, they can borrow an unlimited number of books (up to 10 books borrowed at any one time,) that are enrolled in the Select program.

Amazon may change its pay structure but at the time of writing, Amazon pays by the number of pages read. The pay rate varies by month, depending on the Select payout pool amount versus Amazon's overall number of borrowed pages read. So far, the pay rate has been about $0.005 per page read. It remains to be seen if the pay rate will remain close to this amount or not.

Borrows could add to your bottom line since borrows do not necessarily cannibalize sales. A reader who borrowed your book may not necessarily have bought your book had it not been part of Kindle Unlimited. Loaning your books may help increase you and your book's exposure to new readers. The benefit of improved exposure is multiplied if you have a backlog of books for new fans to buy or borrow.

The downside to joining Select is that it prevents you from publishing your book on other platforms like iTunes, Google Play, Nook and Kobo. Kobo is currently more popular than Amazon in Canada so if your books are Canada-sentric, you might not want to consider joining the Select program. Uploading your book to other publishing platforms goes beyond the scope of this book.

Every book is different. Some may benefit more from being enrolled in Select rather than being offered for sale on other platforms. The reverse may be true for other books. If you are new to self-publishing, I suggest enrolling your book in Select for at least the first 90 days to try it out. It is easier to go exclusive before you are published on many other platforms than have to un-publish on all the other platforms so that you can become exclusive to Amazon.

Uploading your book onto each new platform poses its own learning curve so I suggest giving yourself some time to learn the ropes of publishing on each of the other platforms. Offering your book on multiple platforms increases your exposure in a different way, since not all readers are on Amazon.

It gives you the opportunity of generating multiple income streams rather than just placing your book in one (Amazon) basket. If you plan to publish books to make money, I think it's wise to not be solely reliant on one selling platform. Be sure to uncheck the KDP auto-enroll option for your book in your bookshelf if you intend to leave Select after your 90-day term is up.

Keywords

Besides your title, subtitle and description, the keyword section is your catch-all where you can add all the search terms that you were not able to include before. Even though Amazon suggests that you can only include up to 7 "keywords", you can actually use key phrases. Using keywords is virtually useless because a word like "vampire" or "sexy" pulls up far too many search hits for your book to ever be found. For example, the "vampire" keyword will give you over 31,000 hits. "Sexy" will yield over 39,000 hits.

Instead, use key *phrases*. If you use the key phrase "sexy vampire", the number of hits drops to a slightly more manageable 900+ hits. Add another word to your phrase, say "sexy teenage vampire" and you that three hits. *Three.*

As indie author, Stella Wilkinson (http://www.stellawilkinson.com/) notes on KBoards, "The key is to find keywords that are popular but not too popular. But remember, it isn't how many people search for those keywords, it is how many hits those keywords produce". That is, you want to use popular keywords but not to the extent that your book gets lost among thousands of other books. On the flip side, you also want to have terms that are not so specific that it does not turn up anything.

Ms. Wilkinson uses what is called keyword stuffing. As an example, she noted that she used the terms "paranormal romance witch werewolf zombies ghost shifter love" to cover all her book's theme bases. You can use word repetition to try to hit as closely to an exact search term as possible.

To help you figure out what key phrases to use, think of what you will type into the Amazon search if you were looking for a book like yours. In fact, Amazon's search box will also help to narrow down popular search terms. As you type your search term into Amazon's search, Amazon will display commonly search-for terms based on your word-choice.

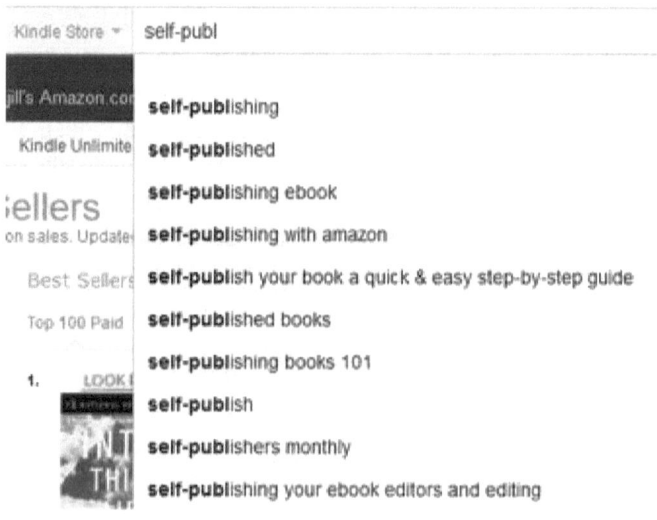

Take some time to do some Amazon keyword searches to find terms that produce a book list of more a few hundred books but less that 5,000 hits. You will need to decide what figure you want to use depending on how big your book's genre is.

To avoid incurring the wrath of Amazon or your potential readers, always use only keywords or phrases that are relevant to your book. Amazon also does not allow you to include names of other authors or book titles (like Harry Potter) in your keywords.

Although Amazon states that you can use up to 7 keywords, as long as you do not include a comma between your words, Amazon will recognize your term as one key phrase. You can include up to 400 characters. Anything extra will be cut-off. Try to maximize the use of the character allotment. Unless you know what you're doing in terms of coding, avoid using any punctuations like hyphens or quotation marks as these will affect the search results and reduce the number of characters you have to use for actual words.

Categories

Key phrases will also help your book get into the categories that you want your book to be in. While you can choose to categories to put your book into during publication, the choices are much more limited than the number of categories that Amazon actually has. For example, if you are publishing a book about frozen desserts and want it to appear in the category "Books > Cookbooks, Food & Wine > Desserts > Frozen Desserts", then you should include that phrase in your keywords. The best way to research categories is to see what categories a popular book that is similar to yours is in. Many people search for books by categories so it makes good sense to pay attention to what categories your book is in.

Book Descriptions

Once you've managed to gain some visibility for your book and have drawn your reader in with your cover, the book description is your next opportunity to reel in that sale. Your description is another chance for your to stuff keywords into it - as long as it's relevant and makes sense when read by human eyes. Remember that you are trying to sell your book to a reader and not simply trying to gain search engine mojo, which is a means but not an end.

In most non-fiction genres, you want your book's description to captivate the reader by posing a problem that they (not you) may have and how your book can help them solve this problem. In fiction on the other hand, the main objective is entertainment. Your blurb should intrigue the reader just enough that makes them want to buy the book and continue reading. It should not, however, reveal too much.

You will need to use HTML coding to properly format your book description. The most important coding you'll need to use would look like this:

Paragraph break <p>
Line break
<i> italics </i>
<b> bold </b>
<ul> bullet points </ul>

DRM

DRM is the abbreviation for Digital Rights Management. When DRM pertains to digital publishing, it is basically additional software that is supposed to stop pirates from making and selling unauthorized copies of your book.

Unfortunately, DRM does little to stop pirates. Instead, it makes it difficult for honest readers to re-download or convert the format to a new device. While most readers don't care if a book as DRM or not, a small but vocal community may refuse to download books with DRM attached. My personal view is that if the reader already bought my book, they should be free to read it on any device they wish. I recommend **not** enabling Amazon's DRM option.

Book Preview

Once you've uploaded your book cover and book file, you can preview how your book will look under section 7: "Preview Your Book" on the initial publishing page. Clicking the "Preview Book" button will launch your book in Amazon's book previewer.

From this previewer, you can

1. Adjust the font size.
2. Skip to any location in the book (Kindle books to not have page numbers).
3. Choose to see how the book will look in a range of different reading devices.
4. Click on the "Book Details" button to take you back to your publishing page.

Once you've reviewed the formatting on the previewer, you can save all your information and continue to the next publishing page. Previewing your book's formatting before publishing is optional but recommended.

On the next publishing page, you can choose to publish your book worldwide, or to only publish in specific territories. Unless you have a reason for publishing only in specific territories, such as if you've already sold some territorial publishing rights, I suggest selecting the "worldwide rights" publishing option.

Royalty Rates

For books priced at under $2.99, Amazon offers a 35% royalty rate exclusive of any VAT (value added tax). That is, for a book priced at $1, Amazon will pay you $0.35 less VAT for sales to European Union countries that charge VAT.

For books that are priced between $2.99 and $9.99, you have the option of choosing the 70% royalty rate. However, Amazon will deduct their delivery charge from this 70%. Delivery charges at the time of writing are:

Amazon.com: US $0.15/MB
India on Amazon.com: INR ₹7/MB
Amazon CA: CAD $0.15/MB
Brazil: BRL R$0.30/MB
Amazon.co.uk: UK £0.10/MB
Amazon.de: €0,12/MB
Amazon.fr: €0,12/MB
Amazon.es: €0,12/MB
Amazon.it: €0,12/MB
Amazon.nl: €0,12/MB
Amazon.co.jp: ¥1/MB
Amazon.com.mx: MXN $1/MB
Amazon.com.au: AUD $0.15/MB

What this means is that the larger your book file is, the more Amazon will charge in delivery fees. An epic book or an image-heavy book that is loaded with high resolution images will have files that are larger in size.

For an extremely large book file, you may be better off going with the 35% royalty rate. However, for most books in general, selecting the 70% royalty rate will effectively net you about 60-65% in royalties after delivery charge.

Kindle Matchbook/Lending

Finally, you have the option of joining Kindle Matchbook and/or Book Lending. Matchbook allows the buyer of your print book to download a digital copy of that book either at a discounted price or for free. Book Lending allows the original purchaser to "loan" their copy of their book to friends or family for 14 days.

I offer my digital books for free under Matchbook and allow lending because I think it's a great way to foster good public relations with your reader. Allowing lending exposes your book to a wider audience at little cost to you. The upside is that you may even gain a fan for your other books after they've read their book loan.

Finally, check the box that confirms that you have the right to publish the book then click the "Save and Publish" to publish. If this is the first book that you are publishing on Amazon, your book will generally stay in the publishing phase for about 12 hours before going live. Amazon will then usually allow your subsequent books to go live more quickly. You can view the process on your KDP dashboard. Note that the 12-hour publishing time is an estimate and that I have had books suck in this stage for over 4 days.

If the process exceeds this period, you should contact Amazon using the "Help" button located on the top right hand corner of your KDP page. Amazon's customer service should be able to work any kinks out for you.

Editing Your Published Content

Once your book is live on Amazon, you'll be able to edit any part of your book's content such as the book's description or price, if you need to. To edit your KDP content, go to your KDP bookshelf and click on the button "...", which can be found on the far right of each book.

Clicking the "..." button will reveal a submenu where you can "Edit Details" of your book, "Edit Rights, Royalty and Pricing" (basically the second page of the KDP process), "Enroll in KDP Select", "Edit Matchbook" options, or you may choose to unpublish your book. Unpublishing your book will remove it from Amazon's system. Unless Amazon changes its system down the road, your book will not lose any reviews that it has earned if you re-publish an unpublished book.

10 TRACKING YOUR SALES

If you are like most indie authors, you may find yourself checking on sales on Amazon often. While you can view your overall sales or sales by book over any 90-day period on Amazon's Reports page, I recommend using Book Report (https://www.getbookreport.com) instead.

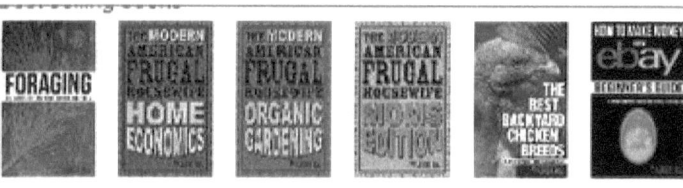

Earnings per day

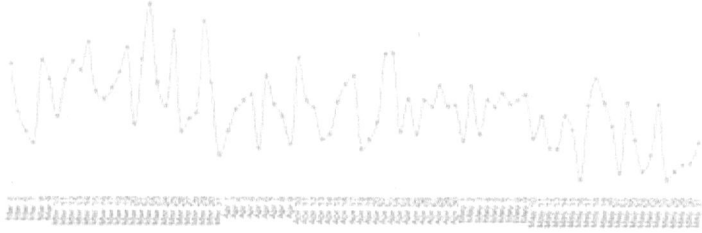

Earnings per book

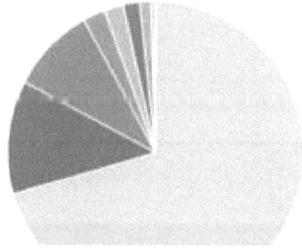

Book Report is free for authors who make less than $1000 a month. If you make more than $1000 per month, the subscription fee is $10. It allows you to see all your sales in neat formats: pie graph, chart and table form. Unlike Amazon, it breaks your sales down by book title and automatically updates as long as you have the window open. It is a wonderful free tool and I cannot recommend it enough.

11 CONCLUSION

Self-publishing can be a fun ride, especially once you get the hang of it and want to write and self-publish more. I will discuss self-publishing on other platforms as well as marketing ideas in future books. However, if you wish to learn about marketing techniques as it pertains to self-publishing now, please join me and other indie authors at the Writer's Cafe on KBoards (http://kboards.com) where we share ideas and indie publishing experiences in an ever-changing self-publishing landscape.

I wish you the best of luck in your journey.

Signup for book updates at http://byjillb.com

Resources

Amazon Direct Publishing (http://kdp.amazon.com)

Word Processing
Microsoft Word (http://www.microsoftstore.com/store/)
Google Docs (http://drive.google.com)
Openoffice (http://openoffice.org)
Wordpress (http://wordpress.com)
Scrivener (http://hyperurl.co/scrivener)
Zotero (https://www.zotero.org/)

Free Classes
Futurelearn (https://www.futurelearn.com)
Coursera (http://coursera.org)

Article Submission Calls
New Pages (http://www.newpages.com)

Editorial Help/Services
Critique.org (http://critique.org)
Scribophile.com (http://scribophile.com)
Critters Writers (http://critters.org)
Book Country (http://bookcountry.com)
Editorial Freelancers Association (http://hyperurl.co/editrate)
Writer's Digest (http://writersdigest.com)
World Literary Cafe (http://worldliterarycafe.com)
Elance (http://elance.com)
Odesk (http://odesk.com)
Fiverr (http://fiverr.com)

KBoards (http://kboards.com/yp).

ProWritingAid (http://prowritingaid.com)
Grammarly (https://www.grammarly.com/)
AutoCrit (https://www.autocrit.com/)

Formatting
Fiverr (https://www.fiverr.com/kindle_format)
Polgarus Studios (http://www.polgarusstudio.com)

Link Shorteners
Bitly (http://bit.ly)
TinyURL (http://tinyurl.com)
SmartURL (http://smarturl.it)

HTML
W3 Schools (http://w3schools.com)
Brackets (http://brackets.io/)
Google Chrome (http://google.com/chrome)

File Conversion
Calibre (http://calibre-ebook.com/)

Cover Design
Canva (http://canva.com)
PicMonkey (http://picmonkey.com)
Pixlr (http://pixlr.com)
Gimp (http://gimp.com)
Fiverr (http://fiverr.com)
KBoards (http://www.kboards.com/yp/)

Adobe Creative Suite (http://adobe.com)

Images

Bucketlistly (http://photos.bucketlistly.com/)

Cupcake (http://cupcake.nilssonlee.se/)

Flickr Commons (http://flickr.com)

Foodie's Feed (http://foodiesfeed.com/)

Getrefe (http://getrefe.tumblr.com/)

Gratisography (http://www.gratisography.com)

ISO Republic (http://isorepublic.com/)

Jay Mantri (http://jaymantri.com/)

Life of Pix (http://www.lifeofpix.com/)

MMT (http://mmt.li/)

Pexels (http://www.pexels.com/)

Picography (http://picography.co/)

Pixabay (http://pixabay.com)

Raumrot (http://www.raumrot.com/)

Re:Splashed (http://www.resplashed.com/)

SplitShire (http://splitshire.com/)

Stok Pic (http://stokpic.com/)

Startup Stock Photos (http://startupstockphotos.com/)

Stock Snap (https://stocksnap.io/)

SuperFamous (http://superfamous.com/)

Wikimedia Commons (http://hyperurl.co/wikicom)

Dollar Photo Club (http://dollarphotoclub.com) only available to old members

Adobe Stock (https://stock.adobe.com/)

1001fonts (http://1001fonts.com)

dafont (http://dafont.com)

Sales Tracking

Book Report (http://getbookreport.com)

Learning More About Self-Publishing

KBoards Writers' Cafe (http://kboards.com)

The Creative Penn (http://creativepenn.com)

JA Konrath (http://jakonrath.blogspot.com/)

Hugh Howey (http://www.hughhowey.com/)

ABOUT THE AUTHOR

A big-city girl who embraced country-living, Jill is a world-traveled Ivy League graduate. She is an entrepreneur, inventor, award-winning writer and author of over a dozen books on homesteading.

In 2011, following the death of a beloved chicken, she co-reinvented the patent-pending Chicken Armor (http://chickenarmor.com) - a chicken saddle/apron which is a device which helps protect the backs of poultry during mating and molting.

She has written articles for various publications including Backyard Poultry Magazino, Farm Show Magazine, Backwoods Home Magazine and Countryside and Small Stock Journal. She has also been quoted in numerous publications including The Associated Press, ABC News, The New York Times, The Washington Times and Yahoo News.

She currently lives in Oregon with her family and menagerie of livestock and hopes that her books will eventually help others to save money, live naturally and to lead a life of self-sufficiency and independence.

Books By Jill b.

Please check out my other books at
http://byjillb.com:

The Modern Frugal American Housewife Book #1
Home Economics

The Modern Frugal American Housewife Book #2
Organic Gardening

The Modern Frugal American Housewife Book #3
Moms Edition

The Modern Frugal American Housewife Book #4
Emergency Prepping

CAN Dos and Don'ts
Water Bath and Pressure Canning

How to Keep Backyard Chickens
A Straightforward Beginner's Guide

The Best Backyard Chicken Breeds
A List of Top Birds for Pets, Eggs and Meat

Foraging
A Beginner's Guide to Wild Edible and Medicinal Plants

Homestead Pepper Garden
10 Herbal Plants for a Survival Medicinal Garden

How to Make Money on eBay: Beginner's Guide

From Setting Up Accounts to Selling Like a Pro

How to Make Money on eBay: Maximize Profits

Secrets, Stories, Tips and Hacks - Confessions of a 16-Year eBay Veteran

How to Make Money on eBay: International Sales

Taking the Fear and Guesswork Out of Doing Business Internationally on eBay

Self-Publishing on a Budget with Amazon

A Guide for the Author Publishing eBooks on Kindle

www.ingramcontent.com/pod-product-compliance
Lightning Source LLC
Chambersburg PA
CBHW021443170526
45164CB00001B/370